V
AND TRIALS FOR WITCHCRAFT IN FIFE

EXAMPLES OF PRINTED FOLKLORE

By

JOHN EWART SIMPKINS

First published in 1914

Read & Co.

Copyright © 2022 Read & Co. Books

This edition is published by Read & Co. Books,
an imprint of Read & Co.

This book is copyright and may not be reproduced or copied in any way without the express permission of the publisher in writing.

British Library Cataloguing-in-Publication Data
A catalogue record for this book is available
from the British Library.

Read & Co. is part of Read Books Ltd.
For more information visit
www.readandcobooks.co.uk

CONTENTS

THE FOLKLORE AND HISTORY OF WITCHCRAFT
An Introduction..5

WITCHCRAFT
Superstitious Belief and Practice........................9

TRIALS FOR WITCHCRAFT 25

THE FOLKLORE AND HISTORY OF WITCHCRAFT

An Introduction

Witchcraft, also called 'witchery' or 'spellcraft' is the use of magical faculties, most commonly for religious, divinatory or medicinal purposes. The belief and the practice of magic has been present since the earliest human cultures and continues to have an important religious and medicinal role in many cultures today. The concept of witchcraft and sorcery, and those accused of its practice have sadly often been utilised as a scapegoat for human misfortune. This was particularly the case in the early modern period of Europe where witchcraft came to be seen as part of a vast diabolical conspiracy of individuals in league with the Devil undermining Christianity. This eventually led to large-scale witch hunts, especially in Protestant Europe. Witch hunts continue to this day with tragic consequences.

Witches and witchcraft have long been objects of fear, and occasionally admiration in traditional folkloric tales. The Ancient Greeks believed in a deity named 'Hecate' who was said to be the god of all witches, as well as hexes, poisonous plants and sorcery. One of the other names she was known by, 'Chthonia' literally translates as 'of the underworld.' Such folkloric beliefs inspired the character of 'Circe' in Homer's *Odyssey*. Here, Circe lived on an island named Aeaea, where she turned passing sailors into wolves and lions. Odysseus only narrowly escaped transformation due to a magical plant. Indian folkloric tradition has an all-together darker tale, that of 'Chedipe'; a woman who died during childbirth. She was said to ride on a tiger at nightfall, and enter people's houses. Then without waking a soul, she would suck the life out of each man through the toes. The most famous English portrayal of witchcraft is the three witches in Shakespeare's Macbeth, inspired by the tale of the Moirai. These three sisters—or fates—are the first characters the audience encounters and act as agents of destruction, sending Macbeth into a spiral of corruption and obsession.

In Early Modern European tradition witches were stereotypically, though not exclusively women. European pagan belief in witchcraft was associated with the goddess Diana, and was fully believed by much of the population. With the advent of Christianity however, such beliefs were dismissed as 'diabolical fantasies' by medieval Christian authors. Early converts to Christianity looked to Christian clergy to work magic more effectively than the old methods under Roman paganism, and Christianity provided a methodology involving saints and relics, similar to the gods and amulets of the Pagan world. The Protestant Christian explanation for witchcraft, such as those typified in the confessions of the Pendle witches (a series of famous witch trials which took place in Lancashire in 1612), commonly involves a diabolical pact or at least an appeal to the intervention of the spirits of evil.

The witches or wizards engaged in such practices were alleged to reject Jesus and the sacraments; observe 'the witches' sabbath' (performing infernal rites that often parodied the Mass or other sacraments of the Church); pay Divine honour to the Prince of Darkness; and, in return, receive from him preternatural powers. It was a folkloric belief that a Devil's Mark, like the brand on cattle, was placed upon a witch's skin by the devil to signify that this pact had been made. The Church and European society were not always so zealous in hunting witches or blaming them for misfortunes. Saint Boniface declared in the eighth century that belief in the existence of witches was un-Christian. The emperor Charlemagne further decreed that the burning of supposed witches was a pagan custom that would be punished by the death penalty. In 820 the Bishop of Lyon repudiated the belief that witches could make bad weather, fly in the night and change their shape. This denial was accepted into Canon Law until it was reversed in later centuries as witch hunts gained force.

It should be noted, that not all witches were assumed to be harmful practitioners of their craft. In England the provision of curative magic was the job of a witch doctor, also known as a cunning man, white witch, or wise man. The term 'witch doctor' was in use in England before it came to be associated with Africa. 'Toad Doctors' were also credited with the ability to undo evil witchcraft. Since the twentieth century, witchcraft has become a designated branch of modern paganism. It is most notably practiced in the Wiccan and witchcraft traditions, which are generally portrayed as revivals of pre-Christian European ritual and spirituality. They are understood to involve varying degrees of magic, shamanism, folk medicine, spiritual healing, calling on elementals and spirits, veneration of ancient deities and archetypes as well as attunement with the forces of nature. Today, both men and women are equally termed 'witches.' We hope that the reader is inspired by this incredibly short history of the folklore surrounding witchcraft, to find out more about this intriguing subject.

WITCHCRAFT

SUPERSTITIOUS BELIEF AND PRACTICE

St. Monans.—Warlocks and all them sort of elves have no shadow.—JACK, p. 94.

Buckhaven.—Witches are the warst kind of devils, they mak use of cats to ride upon, or kail-kebbers [cabbage-stumps], and besoms, and sail over seas in cockle-shells, and witch lads and lasses, and disable bridegrooms.—GRAHAM, p. 236.

Aberdour—I have myself conversed with an old woman who accounted for the lameness of an ancient crone, whom she had in her childhood seen, by an injury she had received when returning from one of her witch journeys. The form she had assumed was that of a black cat; and when she was about to enter her house, through a broken pane, a man passing with a hedge-bill in his hand, struck the animal on the leg, and the witch was lame ever afterwards.—ROSS, p. 327.

Carnock.—At Loanside lived a witch noted for calling up the spirits of the dead, and prophesying the movements of the living, transforming herself at will into inconceivable shapes, such as a March-hare. As an illustration of the Gled's power, a cow was grazing on the Clune road, and, slipping her hand over its back as she passed, it was observed from that hour its udder withered and ceased yielding any more milk. If she happened to spy a *kirning* it would yield or not yield butter as she "wished." Adam Dale, a well-to-do farmer of Bal, actually consulted and obeyed her as to remedies for ills that cattle and folk are heir to, and like "Endor" of old, could hold the cat and play kitlin.

On his last visit, a cinder sparked out of her fire in the form of a coffin, and he never again returned, but died shortly after.

ALLAN, pp. 29, 30.

Dunfermline.—Auld Bessie Bittern . . . was regarded as one who was "no very canny," and whom it was unsafe to disagree or to meddle with, and whose curses or prayers were equally to be dreaded. Even her big black cat did not escape suspicion. . . . One day Bessie appeard at the side of Johnnie K.'s loom, and said to him, "Johnnie, ye'll gang the morn and howk my wee pickle tatties—eh?" "Deed an' he'll do naething o' the kind," shouted Kirsty, his wife from the kitchen, "He has mair need to dad awa' at his loom, an' get his cut oot." Bessie replied, "He'll may be no get his cut oot any the sooner for no howkin' my wee pickle tatties." "Ye'll better let me gang," said Johnnie to his wife, in a submissive tone. "Ye'll no gang your tae length," said Kirsty. "Ye auld neer-be-gaun jade, an' ye'll no let him howk a wee pickle tatties for a puir auld body like me! Ye'll no be ony the richer for't, I weell a wat! Noo mind ye, I'm tellin' ye!" shouted Bessie, as she toddled out of the shop, followed by her black cat.

Johnnie had scarcely resumed his work, when out flew his shuttle, and fell on the floor. He got off his loom and lifted it up, and then tried again, but with a like result. Out it sprang once more, giving him the trouble and delay of going for it, and lifting it with a sad, sorrowful heart, and a deep sigh. He considered himself bewitched, and it appeared as if a "judgment" had come upon him sooner than he expected. He then, as his only resource, took the shuttle to the kitchen, and sitting down before the fire . . . in order to break, if possible, the spell that hung over him, he began by solemnly drawing the shuttle three times through the smoke, dolefully saying as he did so, "I kent hoo it wad be, I kent hoo it wad be! "He then turned to his wife and said, "O Kirsty! ye micht hae mair sense than contrar' that auld witch Bessie Bittem."—STEWART, pp. 143, 144.

Interior of Fife.—An aged woman, bearing the character of a witch, lived alone in a miserable hovel, situated on an extensive moor in the centre portion of Fife. Besides bearing the notoriety of being an "uncanny wife," she was celebrated in the district for a wonderful breed of "doos" (pigeons) which she reared. On a certain day a boy made his appearance at the old woman's hut, and desired to purchase one of these pigeons. Being supplied according to his wishes, he turned his steps homewards, but had scarcely gone a mile when he discovered that the pigeon had disappeared. Scarcely knowing what he did, he returned to the old hag's hovel, where on entering he beheld his own bird sitting amongst its kin. An altercation immediately ensued betwixt him and the old woman, but he eventually regained possession of the bird, which this time he carried home in safety. Next morning, however, it was nowhere to be seen, and, after a search, was again discovered in the witch's hut. The boy's parents, by this time becoming suspicious that there had been some supernatural agency employed in this miraculous disappearance, applied to another old woman for aid, who advised them to send their boy to the witch's habitation, who, unseen, should cut off a small portion of her petticoat, which, on the boy's return, should be thrown into the fire. This was done. No sooner had the rag caught fire than a great noise was heard, and the old witch appeared at the doorway. Exclaiming that they were burning her heart, she rushed forward, seized the flaming fragment from the hearth, disappeared, and was never again seen in that district.

D. D. A., p. 83.

Isle of May.—There is a light-house upon the isle . . . [on] a tower fourty feet high.

(Note.)—The unfortunate architect to the tower was drowned on his return from the isle, in a storm supposed to have been raised by some still more unhappy old women, who were in consequence burnt as witches.

SIBBALD, p. 100; N.S.A., vol. ix. p. 612.

Newburgh.—In the beginning of the present century a reputed witch named Jean Ford was living in Newburgh. The belief in her occult powers was so strong, that sailors before setting out on a voyage were accustomed to propitiate her with a present to ensure a safe return. Jean in her latter years, was warned to remove from her house by her landlord, who had no dread of her hidden powers; not so, however, his wife. After receiving the notice of removal, Jean went to the landlord's residence (and taking care to stand where she could be seen by the inmates), she began to make mystical signs on the ground with her staff, muttering all the while some words to herself. The servants who had a wholesome dread of her powers, attracted the attention of their mistress towards her. The spell was successful; the warning was removed, and Jean was allowed to remain in her house all her life.—LAING, p. 381.

St. Andrews.—In the first half of the nineteenth century it was alleged that a woman in the village of Strathkinness on the last night of the year skipped in the open air swinging a cow-tether made of hair over her head while she repeated:

"Hares' milk, and mares' milk,
An' a' the beas' that bears milk,
Come to me!"

Her cow's tail being diseased, she examined that of a neighbour, which afterwards rotted away while hers recovered. A wounded hare took refuge in her garden, and she was afterwards seen with her head bandaged. Somewhat earlier another witch used to enter Clermont Farm during churning, which checked the process. A ploughman put a sixpence in the churn, and when the witch stooped to light her pipe, he pressed the churn-staff hard on it. She could not raise her head till he moved it. [Abstract of note by Dr. D. Hay-Fleming in *Folk-Lore*, vol. ix. p. 285.]

WITCHCRAFT AND TRIALS FOR WITCHCRAFT IN FIFE

Sir Michael Scott of Balwearie.—Sir Michael Scott of Balwearie . . . was dubbed a knight by King Alexander III. (of Kinghorn memory) for good service done as ambassador at the Court of France, . . . Sir Michael demanded in name of his master, certain concessions which the French King refused. Balwearie desired him to think the matter over, until the black horse which he rode should stamp three times. Stamp number one set all the bells in France a-ringing. Stamp number two of the coal-black steed threw down some towers of the palace. The French King did not wait to see what would be the effect of stamp number three. . . . He had no end of 'pacts with the devil. One demon he bought with the loss of his shadow. A Fife Laird—a wee Fifish[1] no doubt—met Sir Michael out hunting shortly after this little transaction, and said Balwearie's personal appearance would be much improved were he to bring his shadow along with him. No sooner had the Laird got out his joke, than he felt his sight grow duller. He went homewards alarmed. But he had not gone far before he became stone-blind, and was killed by falling over a precipice.

In a sweet little dell, a short way south-west from the ruined Tower of Balwearie stands a singular mass of sandstone, a conspicuous object in the landscape known as the Bell Crag. Tradition says that once Sir Michael rode his black steed (his Paris friend) to the top, having occasion to summon his vassals together, and that the infernal animal indented the rock with a deep and distinct hoof mark.—FARNIE, pp. 62-63.

Sir Michael occasionally intermitted his severer studies to enjoy the pleasures of the chase. When hares were scarce, or did not sit close, he had recourse to an old woman, who inhabited a cottage on his property, and who in consideration for the protection extended towards her, condescended to become puss in such emergencies, and give the dogs a turn or two for the amusement of their master. In these diversions, the old lady always eluded their pursuit. It happened, however, one day that a stranger hound belonging to one of the party was in the hunting field; but as he was held in leash, Sir Michael did not hesitate to start Lucky as usual. Just as the hare was beginning to gain upon her pursuers some one cut the leash which held the strange dog. Off started the hound fresh from the springs, and soon overtook poor puss. By this time, however, she was close to a hut on the moor, which she was observed to enter, by leaping through a bole, or small open window, in the gable. But she did not effect her escape till she had been slightly wounded by the stranger dog; and it was remarked by the neighbours that Lucky had a limp ever after, which incapacitated her for enacting the part of puss for the amusement of the wizard and his guests.

He was hunting one day, when, feeling hungry, and spying a house not far off, he sent his servant to ask a cake of bread. The gudewife replied she had no bread in the house, while the blazing fire, the reeking girdle, and peculiar savour of burnt meal, so grateful to the olfactories of every Scotsman, assured him that she had told a falsehood. Quitting the inhospitable mansion, he returned to his master and stated the result of his mission, and the observations he had made. Sir Michael, taking a devil's buckie[2] from his pocket, gave it to his servant, and desired him to return to the farm-house, and place it unobserved above the lintel of the door. No sooner had he done so than the charm began to work. The auld wife "ayont the fire" was seized with an ungovernable fit of dancing, which consisted in rapid gyrations around the chimney—chanting at the same time, as loud as could reasonably be expected from the lungs attached to members executing the Highland Fling:

"Sir Michael Scott's man
Came seekin' bread and gat nane."

In the meantime, the farmer began to wonder why his spouse had neglected to send the shearers' dinner to the field, and so dispatched an emissary to ascertain the reason. The girl no sooner crossed the threshold than she was seized with the spirit of St. Vitus, and began to caper round the cradle chimney on a footing of perfect equality with her mistress, and with a vehemence which made her think a kemp,[3] or even the barrel-ride, very gentle exercise compared with it. The messenger not returning, the gudeman resolved to solve the mystery himself, and walked towards the homestead. . . . Before entering the kitchen, however, . . . he resolved to reconnoitre through the window, . . . when he beheld his better half and her handmaiden dancing like five-yearaulds. Determined to punish them for such flagrant indecorum, he entered the house, but no sooner had the devil's buckie sounded in his ears than . . . with old-fashioned gallantry he whisked off and joined the ladies. The high dance, commenced by a single performer, had now become, by repeated accessions, a most uproarious threesome reel, enlivened by the inhospitable matron chanting, in a voice now getting feeble from exhaustion:

"Sir Michael Scott's man
Came seekin' bread and gat nane."

The wizard . . . sent his servant back to the enchanted house in the course of the afternoon to remove the charm from the door-head. This being done, the three performers dropped from sheer exhaustion upon the hearth [where they fell into a long slumber].—GARDINER, pp. 65-67.

Sir Michael had dispatched this indiscreet person [his serving-man] to the Eildon Hills for his magic book, which had been lent to a potent necromancer who wonned in these parts. He was compelled to swear, before he set out on his important mission, that he would not open the clasps of the mystic volume. His curiosity was too powerful, however, to be restrained either by his faith or fears; and when he had reached the Haughmill, which is near his master's residence, he availed himself of the seclusion of the spot to take, what he had long meditated, a sly peep into the folio, about which Sir Michael and his brother wizard affected so much mystery. No sooner had he opened the volume than a swarm of fiends started out from between the leaves, and became quite clamorous for employment, crying out to the astonished courier whom they surrounded, "Work, work," Here . . . seeing the Windygates hill straight before him, and remembering . . . the many toilsome ascents he had made in executing his master's errands, he conceived the patriotic project of employing the disaffected multitude around him in the task of cleaving the hill in twain. He had scarcely had time to congratulate himself on his ingenious device, by which he had dismissed the infernal legion, when back they sallied, as importunate as ever, exclaiming, "Work, work," and, on looking east, he observed their task was already finished, and in the most masterly manner. There was no resisting . . . as they very plainly indicated that, in the absence of other employment, they would be under the necessity of falling upon their master, and might make cat's meat of him, as it was foreign to their nature to be idle. . . . To manufacture ropes out of sand . . . was the next job assigned to the infernal imps; who were accordingly packed off to Kirkcaldy beach, which furnishes, . . . a plentiful supply of the raw material. But although they were able to achieve wonders, they could not accomplish impossibilities, and so after an unsuccessful attempt at rope-making with such refractory materials, the demons returned in very bad humour to the terrified valet, and demanded more rational employment. . . . He now began to repent his temerity; the fiends being about to tear him in pieces merely to relieve their ennui, when Sir Michael himself most opportunely arrived at the scene of action. With a spell he at once inclosed the demons within their vellum receptacle, excluding only one fiend, who was forthwith dispatched through the air to Padua with the faithless messenger, with instructions to deliver him over to the Doctors of the Infernal College, to be punished for presuming to practice *diablerie* without a diploma.

GARDINER, pp. 67-68.

Kirkcaldy.—Michael Scott, the warlock of Balwearie . . . was troubled with an evil spirit some say the devil himself, who came every night seeking work to do. After performing unheard of exploits and tasks at Sir Michael's bidding, that afflicted mortal at last got relief by giving the demon a task which proved even too hard for him. If this was the scene, it would be down there on these very Kirkcaldy sands that the demon laboured, and laboured in vain (perhaps still toils), trying to make ropes out of sea-sand.

KILROUNIE, pp. 23-24.

The "warlock" doings near Melrose, which were ascribed to Sir Michael are very similar to those which are told of him in Fife. "He cleft Eildon hills in three." This work of cleavage he also practised in the neighbourhood of Kirkcaldy. That den [ravine] which runs up from the town, and which the railway crosses near Dunnikeir foundry, was produced by Sir Michael. He had offended a fiend, and was pursued by him. To stop the pursuit, or get in advance of his enemy, the wizard caused the earth to yawn at that spot, and its yawning mouth has never since been closed . . .

Local tradition connects the road which leads up to Balwearie with Sir Michael. It is generally said to have been his making, very likely, in engineering it he had taken advantage of the opening in the Windygate or West Mill Brae, for the sake of having the road easier. But this simple act of engineering skill popular superstition converted into a work of wizard power, and the intersection is said to have been accomplished by demons.— TAYLOR, vol. ii. pp. 62-63.

Earl Beardie. *Lordscairnie Castle.*—The ancient seat of Earl Beardie,[4] who, according to legendary lore, may still be seen on the last night of the year playing cards with the devil in some corner of the ruin, if one only has the luck to look in at the stroke of twelve.—*F. H. & J.*, 20th July, 1904.

Archbishop Sharp. 1679.—[After the murder of Archbishop Sharp] they took nothing from him but his tobacco-box and Bible, and a few papers. With these they went to a barn near by. Upon the opening of his tobacco-box a living humming-bee flew out. This either Rathillet or Balfour called his familiar, and some in the company not understanding the term, they explained it to be a devil. In the box were a pair of pistoll balls, parings of nails, some worsit or silk, and some say a paper with some characters, but that is uncertain.

KIRKTON, p. 421, *note*; MACKAY, pp. 147-148.

John Knox. Raising the Devil, 1570.—While the venerable reformer lived at St. Andrews, it was rumoured, and very generally believed as a serious truth, that he had been banished from the town, "because in his yard he had raised some sancts, among whom came up the devil with horns; which, when his servant, Richard Bannatyne, saw, he ran wod [mad] and so died." It is stated that Lady Hume and some others thronged round the postman of St. Andrews, with anxious inquiries whether it was true that Knox was banished from St. Andrews, and that Bannatyne had run mad in consequence of seeing the devil raised.

CHAMBERS (2), vol. i. p. 70.

Rosicrucians. *Cupar.*—Lord Fountainhall in his collections of *Decisions of the Court of Session*, vol. i. p. 15, gives the following account of the schoolmaster's encounter with the disciples of the Rosy Cross: As for the encounter betwixt Mr. Williamson schoolmaster of Cupar . . . and the Rosicrucians, I never trusted it till I heard it from his own son, who is at present (1678) minister of Kirkcaldie. He tells that a stranger came to Cupar and called for him, after they had drunk a little, and the reckoning came to be paid, he whistled for spirits; one in the shape of a boy came, and gave him gold in abundance, no servant was seen riding with him to the town, nor enter with him into the inn. He caused his spirits next day bring him noble Greek wine from the Pope's cellar, and tell the freshest news from Rome; then trysted Mr. Williamson at London, who met the same man in a coach near to London bridge, and who called him by his name, he marvelled to see any one know him there, at last he found it was his Rosicrucian. He pointed to a tavern, and desired Mr. Williamson to do him the favour to dine with him at that house, whither he came at twelve o'clock, and found him and many others of good fashion there, and a most splendid and magnificent table, furnished with all the varieties of delicate meats, where they were all served by spirits. At dinner they debated on the excellency of being attended by spirits, and after dinner they proposed to him to assume him into their society, and make him participant of their happy life; but among the other conditions and qualifications requisite, this was one that they demanded, his abstracting his spirit from all materiality, and abandoning and renouncing his baptismal engagements. Being amazed at the proposal, he falls a-praying, whereat they all disappear and leave him alone. Then he began to forethink what would become of him if he were left to pay for that vast reckoning, not having so much on him as would defray it. He calls the boy, and asks what has become of these gentlemen, and what was to pay? He answered, there was nothing to pay, for they had done it, and were gone about their affairs in the city. This relation his son affirmed to be truth.

LEIGHTON, vol. ii. p. 25; HERALD, p. 40.

Punishments for Witchcraft. *Culross*, 1684.—

Oct. 18th, 1684.

Sir . . . I shall informe you, with three remarkable Stories which may be attested by famous Witnesses, many of which are yet living.

I had the curiosity, when I was a Scholar to pass over from

Borrowstonness to Culros, to see a notable Witch burnt. She was carried to the place of Execution in a chair by four men, by reason her Legs, and her Belly were broken, by one of the Devils cunning tricks which he plaid her. This woman was watched one night in the Steeple of Culros, by two men, John Shank a Flesher and one John Drummond, who being weary went to another Room, where there was a Fire, to take a Pipe. But to secure her, they put her Leggs in the Stocks, and locked them, as well as might be. But no sooner were they gone out of the Room, but the Devil came into the Prison, and told her he was obliged to deliver her from the shame she was like to suffer for his sake; and accordingly took her out of the Stocks, and embracing her, carried her out of the Prison. At which she being terrified made this exclamation by the way, O God whither are you taking me! At which words, he let her fall, at the distance from the Steeple, about the breadth of the street of Edinburgh, where she brake her Leggs and her Belly. I saw the impression and dimple of her heels; as many thousands did, which continued for six or seven years upon which place no Grass would ever grow. At last there was a stone dyke built upon the place.

* * * * *

The Author of this letter is a Person of great honesty and sincerity. From the First Relation of his, we have an evident instance that the Devil can transport the Bodies of men and Women thorow the Air; 'Tis true, he did not carry her far off, but not for want of skill and power. Neither was he afraied to hear the name of God spoken; but purposing to destroy both the Soul and the body of the poor creature, he has pretended so much, to excuse himself, at her hand.

The first Story puts me in mind of one Craich a Witch put in prison, in the Steeple of Culross, to whom several years agoe, Mr. Alexander Colvil, Justice Depute came, a gentleman of great sagacity and knowledge as to Witches. He asked if she was a Witch. She denyed. Dar you hold up your hand and swear that you are not a Witch. Yes sir said she. But behold, what a remarkable Judgement of God came upon her. While she is swearing with her arm lifted up, it became as stiff as a tree, that she could not pull it in again, to the amazement of all that were present. One person yet living there, was a witness and can attest this. The Gentleman seing the vengeance of God upon her for her wickedness falls down presently upon his knees, and entreated the Lord in her behalf, who was graciously pleased to hear him.

SINCLAR, pp. 207-212.

Culross.—The mark of a witch's foot is still pointed out on the turret-stair leading to this apartment [on the first floor of the church-steeple], and is reported to have been made by one of these unfortunate women.—BEVERIDGE (2), vol. i. p. 203.

Dysart.—The Red Rocks was the place where reputed witches were burnt.—CHAPMAN, p. 27.

Earlsferry.—The rocks in the middle of the bay are called the Cockstail or Cucks-stool; . . . are said to have got their names from being used as a ducking place for scolds.

CHAPMAN, p. 24.

Newburgh.—In regard to the Cross of Mugdrum, even tradition ceases to furnish any information. . . . It continues to preserve the memory of the spot, in the lands belonging to the town of Newburgh, on which more than one unfortunate victim fell a sacrifice to the superstition of former times, intent on punishing the crime of witchcraft.

O.S.A., vol. viii. p. 177.

St. Andrews.—Near where the Martyrs' Monument now stands, there was formerly a small knoll known as Methven's Tower. This knoll, it was believed, was haunted by the fairies; and on it, too, witches are said to have been burned.... According to tradition, the suspected witches were thrown into the Witch Lake, to see whether they would float or sink. A real witch would not drown, and was therefore burned.... Before being cast into the water, the right thumb of the suspected was tied to the great toe of the left foot, and the left thumb to the big toe of the right foot—otherwise the proof was not canonical, the accused not being crossed.—FLEMING (2), p. 89. Cf. LYON, vol. ii. p. 56, who states that the knoll was called Witch Hill.

St. Monans.—The tradition respecting Witch Grizzie of the fifteenth century; who, having been found guilty of a fatal incantation, was condemned to expiate her guilt in the midst of the flaming faggots. But, during the interval which preceded the execution of the sentence, she was incautiously permitted to fall under the drowsy dominion of Morpheus; and the very instant that her eyelids came in contact with each other, she vanished, with a sonorous noise, in the shape of a droning beetle; and that insect is known by the title of the Deil's Horse to this day. Though Grizzie never after rendered herself visible in human shape, yet those who were mainly instrumental in procuring her condemnation were constantly infested with a droning noise in their ears, whilst every action of their subsequent lives is said to have been governed by enchantment. And since this untoward event, no witch, after condemnation, was suffered to fall asleep.

JACK, pp. 62, 63.

FOOTNOTES:

[1] *Fifish*. Somewhat deranged.—*Jam. Dict. Sup.*

[2] Devil's buckle, the whelk. The East Coast Scots will not eat them, owing to their resemblance to snails.

[3] A strife in the harvest-field, when the reapers try to outdo one another.

[4] Alexander, 4th Earl of Crawford, died 1453. Burke's *Peerage*, 1912.

TRIALS FOR WITCHCRAFT

1563. *Dunfermline.*—Jun. 26 Agnes Mulikine, alias Bessie Boswell, in Dunfermeling, wes Banist and exilit for Wichecraft.[1] —PITCAIRN, vol. i. part I, p. 432.

1572. The 28th of Apryle thair was ane witche brunt in St Androis, wha was accused of mony horrible thingis, which scho denyed; albeit they were sufficientlie proven. Being desyred that scho wold forgive a man, that had done hir some offence (as scho alledged), refused; then when ane vther that stude by said, gif scho did not forgive, that God wald not forgive hir, and so scho suld be dampned. Bot scho not caren for hell nor heawin, said opinlie, I pas[2] not whidder I goe to hell or heawin, with dyvers vtheris execrable wordis. Efter hir handis were bound, the provest causeth lift vp hir claithis, to see hir mark that scho had, or to sie gif scho had any thing vpon hir I can not weill tell, bot thair was a white claith like a collore craig[3] with stringis in betuene hir leggis, whairon was mony knottis vpon the stringis of the said collore craig, which was taken from hir sore gainst hir will; for belyke scho thought that scho suld not have died that being vpon her, for scho said, when it was taken from hir, "Now I have no hoip of myself."—BANNATYNE, p. 339.

18th Januarii 1575. The quhilk day, Robert Grub yownger in Baalye, witnes, examinat, upon the dilatioun and accusatioun of Mariorye Smyht, spous of Johne Pa, dilatit and accusat of wichecraft, sworne, deponis that he hard be his awin wyffe, Isobel Johnestoun, and Nannis Michell, report that the said Isobel Johnestoun, being in traveling of hir childe, Pais wyffe cam to hir and Nannis Michel being thair layit hir hand on the said Nannis, and sche becam seik incontinent thaireftir; and the deponentis wyffe being laid up in hir bed, sche tuik the said Nannis be the hand, and sche becam weil again, and eat and drank witht the rest of the wemen [that] war thar; and attour,[4] deponis that viij or nyne dayis taireftir his spous foirsaid, being verry seik, send for the said Pa wyffe, and sche refusit to cum quhil the deponent yeid hym self and compellit hir to cum, and at hir cumin sche tuik the deponentis wyffe be the arme, and grapit hir, and pat up hir fyngaris betwix the scheddis of hir hair, and incontinent thaireftir sche cryit for mait: and attour, deponis his wyffe was sa seik that nane trowit hir lyffe being oppressit with swait and womyng,[5] quhil Pa wyffe cam and handillit hir, and this was foure yeir syne cum Witsunday.

Christiane Methtuen, . . . deponis in hir aitht that tyme foirsaid sche was present in Grub hows, quhen his wyffe was travelling in hir childe-evill, and Nannis Michel cam in, and eftir sche had askit at Grub wyffe hir ant quhow sche did, Pa wyffe said, sche wald be weil belyffe, and incontinent thaireftir the said Nannis Michel becam verry seik, and Grub wyffe was lychtar[6] incontinent and softer of hir seikness; and Grub wyffe being laid up in hir bed the said Nannis becam the better: and confessis that they war all fleyit,[7] and ane myst cam ower the deponent's ein, that sche could not see quhat Payis wyffe did to Grub wyffe: and forthir deponis that ix days eftir the said Grub wyffe was lychter and being verry seik, the deponent and Robert Grub yeid for Pa wyffe, and compellit [hir] to cum and vesy[8] Grub wyffe, and eftir sche tuik Grub wyffe be the hand sche becam the bettir and eit and drank . . .

James Gilrwitht, witnes, confessis that his kow gaif na mylknes, and his dochtir repruffit and accusit Mariory Smyth that hir fathir kow gaif na mylk, and thaireftir his dochtir becom seik, and Mariory being callit to James Gilrwitht hous to vesy his dochtir, sche said nathyng wald aill hir scho wald be weil aneucht.

Item, Andro Sellar and Thomas Christie, examinat in the

said mater, deponis that they desyrit Johne Pay nocht to depart of the town gyf his and his wyffs caus war gud. He ansuered that he feared, and thairfoir he and his wyffe yeid thair wayis: And Besse Hereis confessed the sam, and forthir [that he] said that for hym self he durst byde: bot yit his wyffe feared, and thairfoir they durst not byde.

FLEMING, pp. 414-416.

1588. *St. Andrews.*—May 28—Alesoun Peirsoun in Byrehill. Dilatit of the points of Wichcraft eftir specifeit...

Verdict. The said Alesoune, being put to the knawledge of ane Assyis of the personis aboue writtin, wes conuict be thair delyverance, of the vsing of Sorcerie and Wichcraft, with the Inuocatioun of the spreitis of the Dewill; speciallie in the visioune and forme of ane Mr William Sympsoune, hir cousing and moder-brotheris-sone, quha sche affermit wes ane grit scoller and doctor of medicin, that haillit hir of hir diseis in Lowtheane, within the toun of Edinburghe, quhair scho reparit to him, being twell zeiris of aige; and thair cuming and gangind be the space of sewin zeiris, quhen scho wes helpit of hir seiknes, quhilk scho had quhan hir poistee[9] and power wes tane fra hir hand and fute; continewing thairby in familiaritie with him, be the space foirsaid; dealing with charmes, and abusing of the commoun people thairwith, be the said airt of Wichcraft, thir diuers zeiris pypast.—(2) Item, for hanting and repairing with the gude nychtbouris and Quene of Elfame[10] thir diuers zeires bypast, as scho had confest be hir depositiounis, declaring that could nocht say reddelie how lang scho wes with thame; and that scho had freindis in that court quhilk wes of hir a win blude, quha had gude acquentance of the Queen of Elphane, quhilk inycht haif helpit hir; bot scho wes quhyles weill and quhyles ewill, and ane quhyle with thame and ane vthir quhyle away; and that scho wald be in hir bed haill and feir, and wald nocht wit quhair scho wald be on the morne: And that scho saw nocht the Quene thir sewin zeir: And that scho had mony guid freindis in that court, bot wer all away now: And that scho wes sewin zeir ewill handlit in the Court of Elfane and had kynd freindis thair, bot had na will to visseit thame eftir the end: And that itt wes thay [these] guid nychtbouris that haillit hir vnder God: And that scho wes cuming and gangand to Sanct Androus in hailling of folkis, thir saxtene zeiris bypast.—(3) Item, conuict of the said airt of Wichecraft, in sa far, as be hir Depositione scho confest that the said Mr Williame Sympsoun, quha wes hir guidschire-sone,[11] borne in Striuiling, his fader wes the Kingis smyth, lernit hir craft, quha wes tanc away fra his fader be ane mann of Egypt, ane gyant, being bot ane barne, quha had him away to Egypt with him, quhair he remanit to the space of tuell zeiris or he come hame agane; and that his fader deit in the meane tyme for opining of ane preist-buik and luking vponne it: And that the said Mr Williame haillit hir, sone eftir his hame cuming.—(4) Item, that scho being in Grange-mure, with the folkis that past to the Mure, scho lay doun seik alane; and thair come ane man to hir, cled in grene clathis, quha said to hir, 'Gif scho wald be faithfull, he wald do hir guid'; and that scho seing him, cryit for help, bot nane hard hir; and thane, scho chargeit him, 'In Godis name and the low he leuit one,' if he come in Godis name and for the weill of hir soull, he sould tell: Bot he gaid away thane, and apperit to hir att ane vther tyme, ane lustie mane, with mony mene and wemen with him: And that scho sanit hir and prayit, and past with thame fordir nor scho could tell;[12] and saw with thame pypeing and mirrynes and gude scheir, and wes careit to Lowtheane, and saw wyne punchounis with tassis[13] with thame: And quhene scho tellis of thir thingis, declarit, scho wes sairlie tormentit with thame: And that scho gatt ane sair straik, the fyrst tyme scho gaid with thame, fra ane of thame, quhilk tuke all the poistic[14] of hir car syde fra hir, the mark quhairof wes blae and ewill faurrit;[15] quhilk mark scho felt nocht, and that hir syd wes far war.[16]—(5) Item, that scho saw the guid nychtbouris[17] mak thair sawis,[18] with panis and fyris: And

that they gadderit thair herbis, before the sone rysing, as scho did: And that thay come verry feirfull[19] sumtymes, and fleit[20] hir verry sair, and scho cryit quhene thay come: And that thay come quhyles anis in the aucht dayes, and when scho tauld last of it, they come to hir and boistit[21] hir, saying, scho sould be war handlit nor of befoir; and that thaireftir thay tuke the haill poistie of hir syde, in sic soirt, that scho lay tuentie oulkis[22] thaireftir: And that oft tymes thay wald cum and sitt besyde hir, and promesit that scho sould newir want, gif scho wald be faithfull and keip promeis; bot, gif sch wald speik and tell of thame and thair doingis, thay sould martir hir: And that Mr Williame Sympsoun is with thame, quha haillit hir and teichit hir all thingis, and speikis and wairnis hir of thair cuming and saulfis hir; and that he was ane zoung man nocht sax zeiris eldar nor hirself; and that scho wald feir quhene scho saw him; and that he will appeir to hir selff allane before the Court[23] cum; and that he before tauld hir how he wes careit away with thame out of middileird: And quhene we heir the quhirll-wind blaw in the sey, thay wilbe commounelie with itt, or cumand sone thaireftir; than Mr Williame will cum before and tell hir, and bid hir keip hir and sane hir, that scho be nocht tane away with thame agane; for the teynd of thame gais ewerie zeir to hell.[24]—
(6) Item, of hir confessioune maid, That the said Mr Williame tauld hir of ewerie[25] seiknes, and quhat herbis scho sould tak to haill thame, and how scho sould vse thame; and gewis hir his directioune att all tymes; And in speciall, scho said, that he tauld hir, that the Bischop of Sanct Androus[26] had mony seiknessis, as the trimbling fewer,[27] the palp,[28] the rippillis[29] and the fiexus;[30] and baid hir mak ane saw[31] and rub it on his chcikis, his craig, his breist, stommak and sydis: And siclyke, gait hir directiounis to vse the zow mylk[32] or waidraue[33] with the herbis, claret wyne; and with sume vther thingis scho gaif him ane sottin[34] fowll; and that scho maid ane quart att anis, quhilk he drank att twa drachtis, twa sindrie dyetis.[35]

Sentence—... There is merely a marking in the margin of the Record, "Conuicta et Combusta."
        PITCAIRN, vol. i. part 2, pp. 161-165.

1588. *St. Andrews.*—17 July ... The quhilk day, conperit Agnes Meluill, dochter of umquhill Androw Meluill elder sumtyme redar at the kirk of Anstrother, born in Anstrother on Margret Wod hir mother, of aige xxxiiij or xxxv yeiris, being delatit as ane suspect of wischcraft...

Item, the said Agnes being inquirit be the minister, in presens of the hail sessioun, convenit with Mr. Thomas Buchannane and Mr. Jhone Caildcluiche and as thai quha ar direct from the Presbittrie, if sche hes skell of persell,[36] syffis,2[37]confort,[38] wormed,[39] aylay-cumpanay,[40] and of ane herbe callit *concilarum*[41] and declaris that sche hes usit syffis, persell, and confort, to help sindry personis that hes hed evill stomokis; and spetialie that sche usit this cuir to Jonet Spens, spous of Jhone Symson in Craill.

Item, being inquirit if sche knawis the vertew of stanis, denyis.

Item, being inquirit quhat vertew is betuix sowth rynnand watter and uther water, knawis nocht, bot heris say south rynand watter suld be usit.[42]

Being inquirit if sche helpit Cathrine Pryde ... in Craill of hir disais and seiknes, ansueris that Cathrine Pryde had ane disais and seiknes, quhilk wes ane consumptioun at her stomak, and that sche maid ane drink of suffis persell and confort, and stipit in aill xxiiij houris, and geif hir to drink, quha drank thairof viij dayis; and thaireftir desyrit hir to wasche hir with waiter and spetialie south rynnand watter; and quhen sche hed weschin hir with the watter, baid hir cast furth the waiter on the midding, for feitt water suld nocht be cassin in ony bodies gait...

Declaris that sche lernit the knawlege of herbis, and spetialie of that herbe *concilarum*, in North Beruik, fra ane man callit Mr Jhone ... and declaris that Mr. Jhone schew to hir that south rynnand waiter is best, and better nor uther watter; and that the samyn is gude to wesche folkis fra the kneyis and elbokis down, and gud to help thair hurt stommok; and sayis that sche hed ane vomeid[43] quhen sche com furth of North Bervik; and that Mr. Jhone lernit hir to tak syffis, persell, and twa blaidis of confort, and *concilarum*, to mak drink of and lernit hir to mak drinkis thairwith.

And forder declaris that Jhone Meluillis wyffe in Craill lernit hir to tak quheit bread with watter and sukker, to help to stanche the vomeid, and sayis sche lernit na uther thing fra na uther persoun.[44]—FLEMING, pp. 620-623.

1597. On the 1st of September there is this other entry in the Register of the Presbytery: "As also a supplicatioun to be maid to his Majestie for repressing of the horrible abuse by carying a witch about; and Mr. Robert Wilichie ordanit to request the magistratis of Sanctandrois to stay the same thair." The witch here referred to was no doubt carried about to detect other witches . . . in all likelihood she was none other than Margaret Aitken, "the great witch of Balwery" . . . (see *Register of Privy Council*, v. 410, *n.*), and so it is plain that at least one Presbytery, despite its zeal against witchcraft, emphatically disapproved of such a method of discovering witches.—FLEMING, p. 801, *note*.

1597. [*Margaret Aitken, the Witch of Balwearie.*]—This summer there was a great business for the trial of witches. Amongst others one Margaret Atkin, being apprehended on suspicion, and threatened with torture, did confess herself guilty. Being examined touching her associates in that trade, she named a few, and perceiving her delations find credit, made offer to detect all of that sort, and to purge the country of them, so she might have her life granted. For the reason of her knowledge, she said "That they had a secret mark all of that sort, in their eyes, whereby she could surely tell, how soon she looked upon any, whether they were witches or not," and in this she was so readily believed, that for the space of three or four months she was carried from town to town to make discoveries in that kind. Many were brought in question by her delations, especially at Glasgow, where divers innocent women through the credulity of the minister Mr John Cowper, were condemned and put to death. In the end she was found to be a mere deceiver (for the same persons that the one day she had declared guilty the next day being presented in another habit she cleansed), and sent back to Fife, where first she was apprehended. At her trial she affirmed all to be false that she had confessed, either of herself or others, and persisted in this to her death; which made many forthink their too great forwardness that way, and moved the King to recall the commissions given out against such persons, discharging all proceedings against them, except in case of voluntary confession till a solid order should be taken by the Estates touching the form that should be kept in their trial.—SPOTTISWOOD, vol. iii. pp. 66-67; CHAMBERS (2), vol. i. p. 291.

1610 Sep. 7th.—Grissell Gairdner . . . of Newburgh. Dailaitit of certane crymes of Witchcraft and Sorcerie . . .

In þe first, for on-laying, be Witchcraft and Inchantment, of ane grevous diseas and seiknes vpone the said Alexander Wentoun; quhairin he lay in a feirful madnes and ffurrie þe space of ten oulkis togidder; and in end, for af-taking of þe said diseas and grevous seiknes of him, be certain directiones gevin, and vþeris devillische practizes vset be hir for his recoverie; committit be hir in the moneth of Februare last bypast. Item, for hir devillisch Sorcerie and Witchcraft, practizet be hir, in laying on the lyk feirfull diseas and unknawin seiknes upone Williame Andersoune wricht in Newburcht, for certane allegit injuries done be him to Andro Baird, his sone; in the quhilk grevous seiknes he continewit the space of ten dayis togidder, tormentit in maist feirfull maner; and af-taking of þe same seiknes, be hir, be repeiting thryse of certain woirds, quhilk scho termet prayeris. And siclyk, for Bewitching of ane kow, pertening to þe said Williame quhairthrow þe haill milk that scho thairefter gaff was bluid and worsam[45] committed be hir devilrie and Inchantment. . . . Item, for þe Bewitching, be hir devilrie and Inchantment of James Andersone, sone to Margaret Balfour in Newburcht, in onlaying of ane grevous seiknes and diseas vpone him; quhairof, in ane grit ffurie and madnes, within foure dayis eftir on-laying þairof, he deceissit; and þairthrow, for airt and pairt of his murthour and deid.[46] . . . Item, for ane cowmone and notorious Witche and abusear of þe people, by laying on of seiknes vpone men, wemen, bairnes, and bestiall; and be geving of drinkis, and vseing of vþer vngodlie practizes, for af-taking of þe saidis seiknessis and diseases, and be consulting with the Devill, and seiking of responssis fra him, at all times this fourtene or fyftene zeir bygone, for effectuating of hir devillisch intentiones . . .

Mr. *Johnne Caldcleuch, Minister*,[47] being sworne maist solemnelie, be the Justice, Deponis, that a fourtene yeir syne this Grissell Gairdner was than suspect to be ane wicket woman, and ane Sorcerer; and be the Depositiones of the Witches execute for Sorcerie and Witchcraft, at Abernethie, Falkland, and Newburcht, scho was reput to be ane manifest Witch; bot becaus thair was na precedent fact qualifeit aganis hir, the Presbiteric thairfoir delayit hir Tryell and accusatioun. And as concerning hir lyfe and conversatioun sen sync, scho hes bene suspect to be ane verne cvill woman; and for hir privat revenge aganis sic as scho buir ony malice vnto, hes vset devillische and vngodlie meanis, be Sorcerie and Incantatioun, to lay on dyuerse grevous diseassis on thame; and speciallie, on the persones set doun in hir Indytement; quhairthrow the cuntrie and parochin quhairin scho dwellis hes bene gritlie sclanderit in suffering sic ane persone vnpwneist . . .

Verdict. . . . The said Grissell to be ffyld, culpable, and convict of the haill crymes aboue mentionat.

Sentence. . . . To be wirreit at ane staik quhill scho be deid; and thairefter hir body to be brunt in asches; and all hir moveabill guidis and geir to be escheit and inbrocht to our soveran lordis use.—PITCAIRN, vol. iii. pp. 95-98.

1623 Aug. 1.—Thomas Greave, Dilaitit of dyuerse poyntis of Sorcerie and Witchcraft following: For cureing of the persones following, be Sorcerie and Witchcraft, to wit: Ane sone of Archibald Arnote in the Wayne, of ane heavie and vncouth[48] sickncs: Ane sone of Andro Geddis in Freuchie, also hevilie disseisit: Ane bairne of Thomas Kilgoures in Falkland, visseit with ane grevous seiknes. Item, ffor cureing, be Sorcerie and Witchcraft, and making of certane croces and singes,[49] off Dauid Chalmer in Lethame, and be causeing wasche his sark[50] in ane South-rynnand watter, and thairefter putting it vpone him; quhairby he ressauit his helthe. Item, ffor cureing of ane woman in Ingrie, besyde Leslie, of anc grcvous seikness, be taking the seiknes of hir and puting it vpone ane kow; quhilk kow thaireftir ran woid,[51] and diet. Item, ffor cureing off Alexander Lausones bairne in Falkland of grit seiknes, be Sorcerie, and making of certane signes, and vttering of dyuerse vnknawin woirdis. Item, ffor cureing of ane woman, duelland besyde Margaret Douglas, of ane grit and panefull seiknes, be drawing hir nyne tymes bakward and fordward be the leg. Item, ffor cureing of Michaell Glassics wyfe, in the Mylnes of Forthe, of ane grevous seiknes, be causing brek ane hoill in the wall, vpone the North syde of the chymnay, and putting ane hesp[52] of yairne thre several tymes furth at the said hoill, and taking it bak at the dur; and thaireftir, causeing the said Michaellis wyfe ix tymes pass throw the said hesp of yairne, and thairby to procure hir help. Item, ffor cureing, be devillerie and Witchcraft, of Williame Kirkis bairne, in Tulliebule, of the seiknes callit *Morbus caducus*,[53] be straiking bak the hair of his heid, taking ane lang claith, with certane vnguent and vther inchantit matter, furth of ane buist,[54] and rowing[55] the bairne nyne tymes within the said claith, vttering, at ilk tyme of the putting about of the claith, dyuerse wordes and croces and vther signes; and be that meanis pat the bairne asleip; and thairby, throw his devillerie and Witchcraft curet the said bairne of the said seiknes. Item, vnderstanding that Johnne Fischer, in Achalanskay, was hevielie diseasit of a grevous and vnknown fever, vpone aduerteisment gevin to him thairof, he causit bring the said Johnne Fischeris sark to him; quhilk sark being brocht, the said Thomas, turning it over, cryit out at that instant, "Allace! the Witchcraft appointit for ane vther hes lichted upone him!" And, luiking at the breist of the sark, he tauld "that the seiknes was nocht cum as zit to his heart." And eftir some croces and signes maid be the said Thomas vpone the sark, delyuerit the sark to Jonet Patoun, the said Johne Fischeris mother, commanding hir, with all speid to ryn to him thairwith; and declairit to hir that "Gif scho come thairwith befoir his heart was assaulted," he should convalese; at quhais cuming to him with the said sark, the said Johnne hir sone was deid. Item ffor practizeing of dyuerse poyntis of Sorcerie vpone Williame Beveridge, in Drumkippie, in Salen, and cureing him thairby of ane grevous seiknes, be causeing him pas throw ane hesp of yairne thre seuerall tymes; and thairefter burning the said hesp of yairne in ane grit ffyre, quhilk turnet haillilie blew. Item, ffor cureing of Margaret Gibsones ky,[56] in Balgonie, be putting thame thryse throw ane hespe of yairne, and casting of certane inchantit watter, inchantit be him, athort[57] the byre; and thairby making thair milk to cum to thame agane, quhilk thay gaff nocht ane moneth of befoir.[58] Item, at Martimes 1621, Elspeth Thomesone, sister to John Thomesone, portioner of Pitwar, being visseit with ane grevous seikness, the said Thomas com to hir bous in Corachie, quhair, eftir fichting and gripping of hir, he promcist to cure hir thairof; and for this effect callit for hir sark, and desyrret tua of hir nerrest friendis[59] to go with him: Lykas, Johnne and Williame Thomesones, hir brether, being sent for, past the said Thomas, in the nicht seasone, fra Corachie towardis Burley, be the space of tuelff myles; and inioynet the tua brethir nocht to speik ane woird all the way; and quhat euir thay hard or saw, nawayis to be effrayed, saying to thame, "it mycht be that thai wald heir grit rumbling, and sic vncouth and feirfull apparitiones, bot nathing sould annoy thame!" And at the ffurde be-eist Burley, in ane Southrynning watter, he thair wusche the sark; during the tyme of the quhilk wasching of the sark, thair was ane grit noyse maid be ffoullis[60] or the lyll beistis,[61] that arraise and flichtered in the watter. And cuming hame with the sark, pat the samyn vpone hir, and curet hir of her seiknes: And thairby committit manifest Sorcerie and Witchcraft. Item, ffor the cureing of Williame Cousines wyfe, be Sorcerie and Witchcraft, be causing hir husband heit the coulter of his pleuch, and cule the samyn in watter brocht from Holy Well of Hillsyde; and thaireftir, making certane conjurationes, croces, and signes vpone the watter, causet hir drink thairof for hir helth; and thairby, be Sorcerie, curet hir of hir seiknes. Item, ffor cureing, be Sorcerie and Witchcraft, of James Mwdie, with his wyfe and childrene, of the fever; and namelie, in cureing of his wyfe, be causeing ane grit ffyre to be put on, and ane hoill to be maid in the North syde of the hous,[62] and ane quick hen4[63] to be put furth thairat, at thre seuerall tymes, and tane in at the hous-dur, widderschynnes;[64] and thaireftir, taking the hen and puting it vnder the seik womanis okstar[65] or airme; and thairfra, cayreing it to the ffyre, quhair it was haldin doun and brunt quik thairin; and be that devillisch maner, practizet be him, curet hir of hir seiknes: ffor the quhilk, the said Thomas ressauit xx lib. fra hir husband. And last, ffor commoun Sorcerie and Witchcraft, practizet be him, and abuseing the people thairby; expres aganis Godis devyne Law, and Actis of Parliament maid agains Sorceraris. . . . Sentence . . . To be Wirreit at ane staik quhill he be deid, and his body thaireftir to be Brunt in asches.—PITCAIKN, vol. iii, pp. 555-558.

1633. Kirkcaldy.—Kirk-Session of Kirkcaldy 1633. September 17th.—The which day compeared Alison Dick, challenged upon some speeches uttered by her against William Coke, tending to witchcraft; denied the samyne . . .

4. Jean Adamson deponed that she heard Alison Dick say to her husband William Coke, "Thief! thief! what is this that I have been doing? Keeping thee thretty years from meikle evil-doing. Many pretty men has thou putten down both in ships and boats; Than has gotten the women's song laid now.[66] . . .

6. Marion Mea son deponed, that she heard her say, "Common thief, mony ill turns have I hindered thee from doing this thretty years; many ships and boats has thou put down; and when I would have halden the string to have saved one man, thou wald not . . .

8. Compeared Janet Allan, relict of umquhile John Duncan, fisher; deponed, that Alison Dick came in upon a certain time to her house, when she was lying-in of a bairn, and craved some sour bakes; and she denying to give her any, the said Alison said, "Your bairns shall beg yet," (as they do). And her husband being angry at her, reproved her; and she abused him in language; and when he strak her, she said that she should cause him rue it; and she hoped to see the powarts [?] bigg in his hair; and within half a year he was casten away, and his boat, and perished.

9. Janet Sanders, daughter-in-law to the said William Coke, and Alison Dick deponed, that William Coke came in to her; and she being weeping, he demanded the cause of it, she answered it was for her husband. The said William said, What ails thee? Thou wilt get thy guidman again; but ye will get him both naked and bare: and whereas there was no word of him for a long time before, he came home within two days thereafter, naked and bare as he said; the ship wherein he was being casten away . . .

12. Compeared Isobel Hay . . . who being sworn, deponed, that . . . the said Alison came into her house, she being furth, and took her sister by the hand, and since that time, the maiden had never been in her right wits.

13. William Bervie declared, that Robert Whyt having once stricken William Coke, Alison Dick his wife came to the said Robert, and said, Wherefore have ye stricken my husband? I shall cause you rue it. The said Robert replying, What sayest

thou? I shall give you as much—you witch. She answered, "Witches take the wit an grace from you," and that same night, he was bereft of his wits.

14. Janet Whyt, daughter of the said Robert, compearing, affirmed the said dittay to be true upon her oath. And added, that she went to the said Alison, and reproved her, laying the wyt of her father's sickness upon her. "Let him pay me then, and he will be better; but if he pay me not, he will be worse. For there is none that does me wrong, but I go to my god and complains upon them: and within 24 hours, I will get a mends of them." The said Janet Whyt declared, that Alison Dick said to her servant, Agnes Fairlic, I have gotten a grip of your guidwife's thigh; I shall get a grip of hir leg next; the said Janet having burnt her thigh before with lint; and thereafter she was taken such a pain in her leg, that she can get no remedy for it, Whilk the said Agnes Fairlie deponed, upon her great oath to be true.

15. Alison Dick herself declared, that David Paterson skipper, having struck William Coke her husband, and drawn him by the feet, and compelled him to bear his gear aboard, the said William cursed the said David and that voyage he was taken by the Dunkirkers. Also, at another time thereafter, he compelled him to bear his gear aboard, and the captain's who was with him; and when the captain would have paid him, the said David would not suffer him; but he himself gave him what he liked. The said William cursed the said David very vehemently; and at that time he himself perished, his ship, and all his company, except two or three. Also she declared, that when his own son sailed in David Whyt's ship, and gave not his father his bonnallie,[67] the said William said, What? Is he sailed and given me nothing? The devil be with him:—if ever he come home again, he shall come home naked and bare, and so it fell out. . .

The same day Alison Dick being demanded by Mr. James Simson, Minister, when, and how she fell in covenant with the devil, she answered, her husband many times urged her, and she yielded only two or three years since. The manner was thus: he gave her, soul and body, quick and quidder full [?] to the devil, and bade her do so. But she in her heart said, God guide me. And then she said to him, I shall do anything that you bide me; and so she gave herself to the devil in the aforesaid words. This she confessed about four hours at even, freely without compulsion...

18. Compeared also Kathrine Wilson, who being sworn, deponed that... Janet Whyt bade her give her [Alison] a plack and she should pay her again: And when she got it, she said, is this all that she gives me? If she had given me a groat, it would have vantaged her a thousand punds. This is your doing, evil tidings come upon you. And she went down the close, and pissed at their meal-cellar door; and after that, they had never meal in that cellar (they being meal-makers). And thereafter, they bought a horse at 40 lib.; and the horse never carried a load to them but two, but died in the butts, *louping to death*, so that every-body said that he was witched...

20. Thomas Mustard being sworn, deponed, that James Wilson going once to sail, Alison Dick came to him, and desyred silver from him, he would give her none; she abused him with language, and he struck her; she said to him, that that hand should do him little good that voyage; and within two days after his hand swelled as great as a pint-stoup, so that he could get little or nothing done with it. The next time also when he was to sail, the said Alison went betwixt him and the boat; and he said, Yon same witch thief is going betwixt me and the boat; I must have blood of her: and he went and struck her, and bled her, and she cursed him and banned him; and that same voyage, he being in Caithness, standing upon the shore, cleithing a tow, and a boy with him, the sea came and took him away, and he died; and the boy was well enough...

In the Minute of 17th December, there is a particular account of the Town and Session's extraordinary Debursements for William Coke and Alison Dick, witches.

Imprimus.—	To Mr James Miller, when he went to Prestowne for a man to try them, 47s	£2	7	0
Item.—	To the man of Culross (the executioner) when he went away the first time, 12	0	12	0
Item.—	For coals for the witches, 24s	1	4	0
Item.—	In purchasing the commission	9	3	0
Item.—	For one to go to Finmouth for the laird to sit upon their assize as judge	0	6	0
Item.—	For harden to be jumps to them	3	10	0
Item.—	For making them	0	8	0
	Summa for the Kirk's part Scots	£17	10	0

The towns part of Expences Debursed extraordinarily upon William Coke and Alison Dick

Imprimus.—	For ten loads of coal to burn them 5 merks	£3	6	8
Item.—	For a tar barrel, 14s	0	14	0
Item.—	For towes	0	6	0
Item.—	To him that brought the executioner	2	18	0
Item.—	To the executioner for his pains	8	14	0
Item.—	For his expences here	0	16	4

Item.—	For one to go to Finmouth for the laird		0	6	0
	summa town part	Scots	£17	10	0
	both	Scots	£34	11	0
	or	Sterling	£2	17	7

O.S.A., Appendix, vol. xviii.

1643. *Pittenweem.*—3d Nov. 1643—"John Dawson has made payment of his grassmail,[68] and of the soume of £40 (£3 6s, 8d. sterling) expenses depursit[69] upon executing his wyff, to the Treasurer."

13th Dec. 1643—" George Hedderwick being found guiltie of giving evil advice to Margt. Kingow, his mother-in-law, captivat for witchcraft, is convict in ane unlaw of 50 merks (£2 15s. 6 1/2d. sterling) and ordainit to mek payment thereof to the Treasurer, to be employed for defraying of hir chairges."

18th Dec. 1643—"Thomas Cook, son to Margaret Horsbrugh, is ordainit to pay three score of pounds (£5 sterling) for expenses depursit on the executing of his said mother for witchcraft."

21st Dec. 1643—"John Crombie is ordainit to pay fourscore pounds (£6 13s. 4d. sterling) for expenses depursit upon Janet Anderson his spouse."

12th Jan. 1644—"Archibald and Thomas Wanderson, and every ane of them, are decerned to pay the soumes of ane hundred merks (£5 11s. 1d. sterling) for defraying of the chairges depursit upon their wives, execut for witchcraft."

COOK, pp. 49-50.

1648. Helen Small, who resided in Monimail parish, had been long reputed a witch; and it was now alleged against her that she had sent to a man in Letham "a stoupfull of barme to be given him to drink whil (*i.e.* till) he was sick," after which he died; that the wife of another man," having flitten[70] with the said Helen, fell sicke," and when the man afterwards reproved Helen, his cow died, and immediately his wife recovered; and that when another man, who was riding to Letham, met Helen, she was heard to say, "Saw yee ever such a long-legged man as this?" after which he fell sick, and" dwined about[71] till he died." The evidence for these accusations, however, taken by the Session of Monimail, proved to be insufficient. Having compeared before the Presbytery, Helen was asked why she was not careful to be purged of this scandal and replied: "that she could not stope their mouthes, and God would reward them."

CAMPBELL, p. 381.

1649. *Dalgety.*—June 3d, 1649—Compears Issobell Scogian and confesses that, having had a sore and vehement paine in her heid since Lambes [Lammas] that Issobell Kelloch, spous to Archibald Colzier, did borrow ane courche [head covering] from her. She off late since the said Issobell Kelloch was blotted [accused] for ane witch, did goe unto her and sought health; wherupone Issobell Kelloch desired her to forgive her, and sate doune upone her knees and said thryse oure, Lord, send the thy health; after which she confessed she was much eased . . . — BUCKNER, pp. 44-46.

1649. *Burntisland.*—Janet Brown . . . was charged in the indictment with having held "a meeting with the Devil appearing as a man, at the back of Broomhills, who was at a wanton play with Isobel Gairdner elder, and Janet Thomson; and he vanished away like a whirlwind.—With having there renounced her baptism, upon which the Devil sealed her as one of his, by a mark on the right arm, into which Mr James Wilson minister of Dysart in presence of Mr John Chalmers minister at Auchterderran, thurst a long pin of wire into the head, and she was insensible of it. . . . The prisoner, and two other women, were convicted, condemned, and executed, in one day.

Within a few days after, other three miserable women arrived at the last stage of a common journey in those days of superstitious ignorance, viz. from the parson of the parish to the criminal judges, and from the criminal judges to the executioner. They were arraigned before the same tribunal, on the hacknied charge of meeting with the Devil. One of them, Isobel Bairdie, was accused of having taken up a *stoup*, *i.e.* a flaggon, and drank, "and the devil drank to her, and she pledging him, drank back again to him, and he pledged her, saying, Grainmercie you are very welcome."—In each of the three indictments, it is added that the prisoner had confessed, in presence of several ministers, bailies, and elders, and . . . that these inquisitors were produced before the court, to prove the *extrajudicial confessions* of the miserable prisoners . . .

ARNOT, pp. 357-359.

1649. *Balmerino.*—March 8.—Elspit Seith, in the paroche of Balmirrinoch, compeiring, is examined by the Presbyterie, and *summond aqud acta* to compeir the next day.

March 15.—The whilk day, Andrew Patrik compeiring, and being examined, declared, that in the last goesommer[72] save one, as he was comming furth of the Galrey to goe to his owne house, betuixt 11 and 12 houres at euen, as he was in the west syde of Henry Blak his land, he saw 7 or 8 women dancing, with a mekle man in the midst of them, who did weare[73] towards him, whil they came to a litle loch, in the which they werre putting him, so that his armes werre wett to the shoulder blaids; and that he knew none of them except Elspet Seith, whom (as he affirms) he knew by hir tongue, for he hard hir say to the rest, "He is but a silly druken larde[74]; let him goe." . . . And that he went in to his owne house with gryt fear all wett. He being questioned, why he did not reveile the foirsaid mater presently theirafter? Answered, that wpon the morn he told it to Alexander Kirkaldy.

Andrew Patrik and she being confronted befor the Presbyterie he affirms, she denyes . . .

August 6th. . . . Elspet Seith is ordeined to be recommended to the Magistrats of Couper to be incarcerat for tryall. The Baillyies are desyred to cause keip hir closse, and permitt no body to offer violence to hir, nor have accesse to hir, but such as the Presbyterie shall appoint . . .

September 13.—This day, Elspet Seith compeires, and being confronted with Jean Bruise, the said Jeane declares, that Elspet Seith had said to her sister, "Is your kow calfed?" The young lasse answered, "Know ye not that our kow is calfed?" The said Elspet replyed, "Their is milk bewest me, and milk be-east, and aill in David Stennous house, and a hungry heart can gett none of it. The Diwell put his foot among it." And before that tyme tomorrow ther cow wold eate none; wherupon they went to find Elspet Seith . . . and desyred hir to come sic their kow. . . . And the said Jean affirmes, that the said Elspet went in to sie the kow, and layd hir hand wpon hir bake, and said," Lamby, lamby, yee wilbe weill enough." And from that tyme furth the kow amended.

It is also declared by the said Jean, that she used to sitt downe in the way when she mett any body.

Isobel Oliphant declares . . . that the said Elspet did cast a cantrep[75] on hir kow, that she wold not eate nor give milk, but did dwyne on a long tyme till she dyed. The said Isobel affirmed, that she never spake it, but Elspet Seith hir selfe did blaze it abroad.

She declares, that she did sitt downe in the gate ordinarily.

Jonet Miller . . . declares, that she came and looked in at Elspet Seithes door, did sie hir drawing a cheyne tether and theirafter the said Elspet tooke the tether, and did cast it east and west, and south and north.[76] She asked hir what she was doing; answered, "I an ewen looking at my kowes tether." The said Janet affirmes, that it is not a yeir since till Mertimes,[77] and it is evidently knowne that she had not a kow this sixteen yeir.

The said Elspet denyes all, and wold have used violence to the said Jonet if she had bein permitted.

Jean Andersone . . . declared, that the said Elspet requyred milk, and she gave her bread but no milk. And when she went to milk her kow, she fand nothing but blood first, and theirafter blak water all that season. . . . She declared also, that the said Elspet used to sit downe when she mett any body.

Andrew Patrik, being confronted with the said Elspet is questioned, if ewer he saw the said Elspet early or late in the fold? Answered, that he had sein hir severall tymes, and once he saw hir in the morning, and he had a little dog who barked despytefully at her: She desyred him, "Stay the dog." He answered "I wold it wold worry yow." Theirafter the dog newer eated. He affirmed also, that he saw hir amongst these women dancing. She denyed all.

. . . . Margaret Boyd is confronted with the said Elspet, and declares, that hir goodman, Robert Broun, went to death with it, that Elspet Seith and other two did ryde him to deathe; which he declared before the ministers wyfe, Mr. James Sibbald, Scholmaster, and David Stennous, elder. She affirms also, that he asked his wyfe, if she did not sie hir goe away? She feared, and answered him, that she saw not; and immediately he was eased.

Jonet Miller againe compeirs, and declares that hir howsband David Grahame, saw Elspet Seith and Helen Young meitt, the one going one way, and the other another, the said Elspet sat downe on hir knees, and Helen Young layd hir hand on hir showlder, and she spak some words to hir. The said David Grahame questioning Helen Young on hir deadbed, what she was doing then when they mate? She answered, that she was desyring Elspet Seith to witch him. He questioned hir, why she wold not doe it hir selfe? She answered, she had no power.

Isobel Blak called, and confronted with the said Elspet, declares nothing, but that she used ordinarly to hurch downe in the gate lyk a hare.

September 20.— . . . This day compeirs Johne Blak, who

declared, that he saw a hare sucking a kow, and she run among the hemp towards Elspet Seith's house.

December 6.—Elspet Seith, in the paroche of Balmirrinoch, suspect of witchcraft, appeiring, the Presbyterie, considering that the town of Couper wold not assist in warding and watching the said Elspet, (according to the Act of Parliament,) and not finding it possible to gett hir otherwyse tryed, having called hir before them, did ordein hir, lykas she promysed to compeir againe when ewer she showld be requyred.

KINLOCH, pp. 136-151.

[Nothing more of this case.]

1650. *Torryburn.*—24th April.—Delated Robert Cusing in Kincardine, who went to the man of Kilbuck-Drummond for ane John Aitkine in Torriburn, for seeking helth to his wyf, whom he allaidged wes witched.

27 of April. Robert Cousing cited, accused of his goeing to the man of Kilbuck, for seeking helth to John Erskin's wyf in Torryburn—denyed altogether that ever he wes employed in such a busines...

30th Apryll 1650. The whilk day John Aitkene being convened befor the session and examined for his alleged consulting with witches anent his wyfe's sicknes, he confessed as follows—that he, hearing a common report that James Young being sick wes healed again by the help of Robert Cousin in Kincardine, went and asked James Young his wyf concerning this; that she bad him goe to Kincardine to Robt. Cousing and hir daughter; that he went to them, and that the said Robert's wyff said to him that hir goodman brought .... from the wyff's son of Kilbuck a yellow gowen[78] which healled hir father; and that the said Robert Cousing agreit with him to go to the said wyff of Kilbuck hir sonne, to get helth to his wyff, that he gave his wyff's much[79] with him, and that he returned with this answeare, that his wyff had gotten wrong by thos whom he suspected; that shee wold be dead befor he went home, that her pictur wes brunt[80] that he brought with him three pieces of rantries,[81] and baid him lay thes onder his door threshold, and keep one of them upon himself with seven pickles of whyt,[82] because seven wes set for his lyf; that he brought with him ane orange-coloured saw,[83] whilk he did keep with himself, because his wyff was dead before he came with it . . .

14 May. . . . This day John Aitken, in presence of Robert Cousing, did affirm that he, hearing report of him that James Young wes healled by a yellow gowan which he brought to him from the wyff of Kilbuk, and that he tok James Young's wyff's much with him; that he came to James Young's hous, and told him his errand. James Young answeared that about bearsyd[84] tyme bygone four years Robert Cousing brought hom a yellow gowan ten myles beyond Dumblane, from Drummond the wyff's son of Kilbuk, and caused him goe to a south-running water and put in his neck and wash himself three times all over in the water, and goe three tymes withersones[85] about, and say, All the evel that is on him bee on the gowen. John Aitkin offered him a firlot of corne and twentie schillings of silver, which he was content with; and that he went away on Saturday in the morning, and returned on Sunday and brought him the rantress, the pickles of whyt, and the orange-coloured saw, and bad him keep a piece of the rantree on him, and put a piece onder his door threshold, for they wer set for his lyf also; and the man told him his wyff wold be dead or he cam home again, bot if shee wer alive to put that saw on hir bak forgainst hir heart, and it wold tak the heat out of it. . . . At length the said Robert Cousing confessed all the premiss *verbatim* as is wreatten. Removed; he is apoynted to mak his repentance in sackcloth, according to the ordinance of the Presbetrie.

BEVERIDGE (2), vol. i. pp. 237-239.

For South-running water see (1588) *Trial of Agnes Melvill*, p. 75. Also pp. 17, 110.

1643. In Fife alone, in the course of a few months of the above year, about forty persons were burnt for witchcraft. Yet singular to say, we have no particulars of these burnings, so common had they become, or so unimportant in the opinion of the nation. The ministers used to thrust, or cause to be thrust, long pins into the fleshy parts of these unhappy women, to try if they were proof against feeling, or to extort confessions from them. At other times, a suspected witch was tied up by the thumbs and whipped, or had the flame of a candle applied to the soles of her feet till she confessed.

LYON, vol. ii. p. 56.

1650. A Witch's Pryer.— . . . 7th May: This day comperit marion Cunnynghame, who, the last day of April 1650, gave in a complaint against Jonet huton, for calling her *witche* and *banisht theef*, whitch complaint was not accepit nor heard, because she did not consign her money for proving the same. Bot the s^d Jonet huton appearand the s^d day and hearing the caus for wch she was cited, Denyit y^t she callit her a witche, bot affirmit y^t the s^d marion *said over a prayer* ilk ny^t quhen she went to hir bed which wes not lawf^l. . . . The s^d Jonet being desyrit to repeat it, affirmed y^t. she had *bot a part yrof*, whitch she said over as follows, viz.:—"*Out throw toothe and out throw tongue, out throw liver and out throw longue, and out throw halie harn pan;*[86] *I drank of this blood instead of wine, thou shall have mutifire [?] all thy dayes syne, the bitter and the baneshaw [?] and manie enil y^t no man knowes.*" Upon the whitch the said marion being askit, denyit the same altogidder . . .

David Lindsay of Cavill gave in a copie of ye s^d marion Cunnynghame's prayer, repeated and said ouer to him be herself as follows:—"*The day is fryday, I shall fast quhill I may; to hear the knell of Christ his bell, the lord god on his chappell stood, and his 12 apostles good. In came Drightine dear lord of Almightine; say man or Ladle sweet St. marie, qt is yon fire so light, so bright, so far furthe fra me; It is my dear sone Jessus, he is naild to the* tre; he is naild weill, for he is naild throw wynegare, throw toothe and throw tongue, throw hail harn pan."... Being posed yrupon, she confest this following viz.—"Out throw toothe and out throw tongue, out throw liver and out throw longue, and out throw the halie harn pan."; but denyit, be the death she must go to, thir words following:—"I drank of this blood instead of wyne, thou shalt have mutifire all thy days syne; the bitter and the baneshaw, and manie evil yt na man knawes."

After other "posings" and "takings" before the Presbytery, she was, until further findings, *suspended from the communion of the Kirk.*—HENDERSON, pp. 321-322,

1650. On the 14th of May 1650, Janet Anderson presents herself before the Session with a bill, in which it is declared that Isobel Inglis and Marjorie Flooker have called her a witch. She craves that the Session will investigate the matter. . . . The appointed day arrives, and the reputed witch and her accusers confront one another, before Mr. Bruce [minister] and the other members of the Kirk-Session. . . . . It is averred that Janet Anderson, coming into the house where Andrew Kellock's child lay in its cradle, put a mitten under its head, and . . . by so doing, she bewitched the child, and caused its death. The witnesses are all put upon oath. Marjorie Flooker depones that she found Janet Anderson's mitten under the child's head after its death, and that she took the said mitten and cast it on the ground. Isobel Inglis depones that she took the mitten, when it was lying on the floor, and cast it into the fire. . . . Isobel further declares that, when Janet Anderson knew that her mitten was burned, she said, "What misters [necessitates] the mitten to be burned, after the bairn is dead: for, if there had been any ill in the mitten, it was past before the death of the bairn." Other witnesses corroborate this evidence; and Andrew Kellock and his wife depone that Janet Anderson told them, that on the very day that Robert Anderson got himself hurt, he had called her "a trumpous (cross-tempered) witch," and her heart "sythed" (glowed with satisfaction) when she saw him coming home in his hurt condition, holding his injured arm "as if it had been a fiddle." Still further it was deponed that James Murray had declared that he was going from Aberdour to Whitchill one night, he heard "ane great guleing[87] voice and dinne, in the hollow of the gait[88] be southold Couras Aiker (the Cross Acre)," which greatly astonished him.... [on advancing he saw] Janet Anderson, on her knees, scraping the ground with both her hands, and uttering the most unearthly cries. He asked her what moved her to do this, and she replied that she could not tell.... William Watson deponed that, after Janet was delated to the Session she said, in his house, "it might be that her spirit zeid (went) forth out of her when she did not know of it.... She was... released from prison; for another notice we have of her is after the lapse of nine years when she applies to the Kirk-session for a "testimonial," or certificate of character, being on the point of leaving the parish. The Session grants the certificate, but are careful to note the fact that "she had been accused of being a witch."—Ross, pp. 325-328.

1651. *St. Monans.*—.... Maggie was arraigned at the bar of the sanhedrim, under the grave charge of being in compact with the Prince of Darkness, by whom she had been guilty of fell deeds, and caused meikle dool[89] and wonder in the neighbourhood.... She pleaded guilty to the charge—confessing the manner in which she became possessed of the familiar spirit, and for what purpose.... The trial was consequently short, the conviction easy, and the sentence divested of all dubicty, viz.:— That ane great pile of faggots be upbigget on the Kirk Hill the morrow morning, after whilk she sail be forth brought and laid thereon, where she sall suffer the pains of devouring fire in face of the noontide sun of heaven, that all may take warning, and avoid sic like affinity, league, or compact with the wicked spirits of darkness. Meanwhile, two sergeants[90] shall watch her with eidence to prevent slumber and escape.... The process of watching was . . . [that] whilst one of the guards, with a large soundinghorn, continued to assail her ears with intermitting blasts in rapid succession, the other assiduously applied the witchgoad[91] in order to test her consciousness. To this strange ordeal was the ill-fated wretch subjected for nearly twenty-four hours, until the erection of the fatal pile was completed, she was then brought forth pinioned, and extended on its summit; when the beadle judiciously applied his lunt,[92] and the whole combustible materials, in a little space, exhibited a most stupendous and appalling conflagration . . .

The pile being consumed, the beadle's next business was to scatter the ashes towards the four winds of heaven, and collect the fragments of the burnt bones which remained, and deposit them in the Brunt Laft, to which allusion is made in another section of this work. This is the last witch that is said to have suffered the flames in the territories of St. Monance, though tradition teems with prodigious exploits performed by such characters long subsequent to this period.

It may be observed in conclusion, that the three ancient elbow-chairs which were placed on the Kirk Hill during the execution, and occupied by the civic authorities, are still in the Town-hall, and occupied by their successors on all judicial occasions.—JACK, pp. 61-64.

1653. *Newburgh*.—In the minutes of the proceedings of the Kirk session of Newburgh, there is a record of the examination of a woman, named Katharine Key, on a charge of witchcraft, and "for cursing the minister." An imprecation from a reputed witch at that period was heard with dread, and was believed to be followed by certain fulfilment; Katharine Key was therefore brought to trial, and but for a concurrence of circumstances favourable to her, she would have suffered the same or a worse fate than Grissell Gairdner . . .

Sep. 11. Compeired Katharine Key denied that she cursed the minister, but that she cursed these who . . . cause the minister debar her [from the communion] ...

The whilk also the minister gave in against her severall points yt had come to his hearing which he desyred might be put to tryel.

"1. That being refused of milk from Christian Orme, or some other in David Orme's house, the kow gave nothing but bluid, and being sent for to sie the kow, she clapped the kow and said the kow will be weil, and theirafter the kow became weil.

"2. That John Philp having ane kow new calved, that the said Katharine Key came in and took furthe ane peitt fyre and yt after the kow became so sick that none expected she would have lived, and the said Katharine being sent for to sie the kow, she clapped the kow, and said the kow will be weill enough and she amendit.

"3. That the minister and his wyfe haveing purpose to take ane chyld of theiris from the sd Katharine which she had in nursing, the chyld wold sucke none womans breast, being only ane quarter old, bot being brought back againe to the said Katharine presently sucked her breast.

"4. That theirafter the chyld was spayned[93] she cam to see the chyld and wold have the bairne in her armes, and yrafter the bairne murned and gratt in the nyght and almost the daytyme, also that nothing could stay her untill she died. nevertheless befoir her coming to sie her, and her embracing of her took as weill wt the spaining and rested as weill as any bairne could doe.

"5. That she is of ane evil brutte and fame and so wes her mother befoir her ...

The accusation contained in the fifth charge of the indictment, that "her mother befoir her was of evil bruit and fame" was of momentous import; judge, jury, and people firmly believing that occult powers descended by blood from mother to child ...

1655. 3d Junii Kathrin Key compeired befoir ye session having been befoir the presb:[94] the minister declaird he was appointed be the presb: to intimati out of the pulpitt anent Kathrin Key if any person had any thing to lay to her charge anent witchcraft, or relating yrto they sould compeir befoir ye session, and yrafter she to be admitted to her repentance for cursing the minister and session if nothing anent the former came in against hir.

10 Junii Ye session sitting, ye beddell was desyred to call at ye church door if yt yt wer any yt had any thing to say against Kathrin Key they sould compeir, he having called 3 severall tymes, and none compeiring ye session appoints her to compeir on the public place of repentance the next Saboth, for cursing the minister and Session...

It is more than probable that the accused was thus leniently dealt with, from the salutary influence of the English judges appointed by Cromwell at this very period to administer the law of Scotland; they having expressed their determination to inquire into the tortures that were used to extort confession from the unhappy victims of popular superstition.

LAING, pp. 223-228.

1675. *Culross*,—Catherine Sands confest that to be revenged of her brother who had wronged [her] in parting of her father's goods, and gear; she was brought under the Devil's service who appeared to her in the likeness of a Gentleman. And in the first place caused her renounce Christ and her Babtism, and give her self over both soul and body to his service by laying one of her hands to the Crown of her head and the other to the sole of her foot &c.... Isabel Inglis confest that... the Devil... caused her resign her self to him... in the way and manner confessed by Catherine Sands. And furder confessed that her spirits name was Peter Drysdale and her name which he gave her is *Serjeant*.

Janet Hendry made the like confession with the two former.... That her spirits name is Lawrie Moor and that the name he gave her is *Major*.

Agnes Hondry confessed... And Declares that her spirit's name is Peter Selanday but remembers not what name he gave her.[95] ... MSS., vol. i. pp. 322-323.

Dec. **1691.** *Dysart* . . . Complains Margaret Halket upon Euphan Logan that the said Euphan did maliciously abuse me in my credit and reputation by calling me a witch, and saying that I bewitched her brewings and several other such expressions; and upon Saturday last, she came to Alexr Laws house and abused me and flew in my throat, and if Alexr Law had not rescued me, she would have destroyed me . . .

Chatherine Cragie being examined, depones that she heard Euphan Logan say that her brewings went wrong, and that she could blame no person but Margaret Halket . . .

Elspeth Mitchell being examined depones—Euphan Logan flew to Margaret Halket's head and that Alexr Law red them; and that the said Euphan said she came to get *blood of her*, and that she heard her at other times call her witch . . .

Fined five pounds Scots, and remain in prison until payment thereof.—MUIR, pp. 54-55.

1701.*Anstruther*,—April **15, 1701.** The Kirk-Session of Anstruther Easter met.—Inter alia—Elizabeth Dick cited, called and compearing confessed she came to Anstruther Miln and sought an alms for God sake but being refused went away, and being sent for a little tyme after to the Miln confessed she saw the meall of an red colour, and that she said God be in the Miln, and sitting down she said God have an care of me for my heart is louping, and presently the Miln went right and the rest of the meall came down white. James Osten, in the Miln being one of the witnesses cited, called and compearing confessed that when he was grinding at the Miln, as the Mill was set on, and a handful of his pease meale ground while Elizabeth Dick being in the Miln immediately after she went out the meale changed its colour and cam down red at which the miller caused grind some sheeling-seeds they came down red also. A little after the meale came to its own colour. . . . Peter Oliphan's wife cited, called and compearing confessed that as he was grinding meall at the Miln Elizabeth Dick came in and sought an alms which she refused, whereupon the above said Dick went away and immediately the Miln went wrong, and the meall turned red, presently she sent for Elizabeth Dick and gave her an handful of the red meale, at which Elizabeth Dick said God have an care of me for my heart is louping and presently the meall turned white and the Miln came right.

The Session thinks fit to refer this entirely to the Presbytery.

MURRAY.

1704. Witch's Confession (from Torryburn Session Records).—Torryburn, 29th July **1704.**— . . .

Lillias Adie being accused of witchcraft by Jean Neilson, who is dreadfully tormented, the said Lillias was incarcerate by Bailie Williamson about ten of the night upon the 28th of July.

Lillias being exhorted to declare the truth, and nothing but truth, she replied, what I am to say shall be as true as the sun is in the firmament.

Being interrogate if she was in compact with the devil, she replied, I am in compact with the devil, and have been so since before the second burning of the witches in this place. She further declared, that the first time she met with the devil was at the Gollet, between Torryburn and Newmilne, in the harvest, before the sun set, where he trysted to meet her the day after, which tryst she kept, and the devil took her to a stook side, and caused her renounce her baptism; the ceremony he used was, he put one hand on the crown of her head, and the other on the soles of her feet, with her own consent, and caused her say all was the devil's betwixt the crown of her head and the soles of her feet; and there the devil lay with her carnally; and that his skin was cold, and his colour black and pale, he had a hat on his head, and his feet was cloven like the feet of a stirk, as she observed when he went from her.

The next time she saw him was at a meeting at the Barnrods, to which she was summoned by Grissel Anderson in Newmilne, about Martinmas, their number was about twenty or thirty, whereof none are now living but herself. She adds, it was a moon-light night, and they danced some time before the devil came on a ponny, with a hat on his head, and they clapt their hands and cryed, *there our Prince, there our Prince*, with whom they danced about an hour.

The next time was at a meeting at the back of Patrick Sands his house, in Valleyfield, where the devil came with a cap which covered his ears and neck; they had no moonlight. Being interrogate if they had any light, she replied, they got light from darkness, and could not tell what that light was, but she heard them say it came from darkness, and went to darkness, and said, it is not so bright as a candle, the low thereof being blue, yet it gave such a light as they could discern others faces. There they abode about an hour, and danced as formerly. She knew none at the meeting but Elspeth Williamson, whom she saw at the close of the meeting coming down by the dyke-side; and she said, she was also at another meeting in the Haugh of Torry, where they were furnished with the former light, and she saw Elspeth Williamson there also.

July 31st, **1704**.— . . . . Lillias Adie adhered to her former confession, and added, there were many meetings she was not witness to, and was at many of which she could give no particular account . . .

Being interrogate if the devil had a sword, she replied, she believed he durst not use a sword; and called him a villain that promised her many good things when she engaged with him, but never gave her any thing but misery and poverty.

The last meeting ever she was at, was 14 days after the Sacrament, in the month of August 1701, upon the minister's glebe where the tent stood, their number was 16 or 18, whereof Agnes Currie was one. She added, that she made an apology to the meeting, because she could not wait upon them all the time, being obliged to go to Borrowstouness that morning's tide. She added, that she heard Jean Neilson was with a devil, and troubled with a fit of distemper, but declared she never wronged her, though the devil may do it in her likeness.

Elspeth Williamson being called, came into the prison where the session sate and being interrogate if Lillias Adie had any envy at her, she answered, she knew no envy she had at her. Lillias being interrogate if Elspeth Williamson was guilty of witchcraft, she replied, she is as guilty as I am, and my guilt is as sure as God is in heaven . . .

August 19. . . . Lillias Adie confessed that after she entered into compact with Satan he appeared to her some hundred times, and that the devil himself summoned her to that meeting which was on the glebe, he coming into her house like a shadow and went away like a shadow. . . . She added, that the devil bade her attend many meetings that she could not attend, for age and sickness; and though he appeared not to her when there was company with her, yet he appeared to her like a shadow, so that none could see him but herself. At another time she said, that when she renounced her baptism, the devil first spoke the words, and she repeated them after him, and that as he went away she did not hear his feet on the stubble.

August 29th **1704**.—Lillias Adie declared some hours before her death, in audience of the minister, precentor, George Pringle and John Paterson, that what she had said of Elspeth Williamson and Agnes Currie was as true as the Gospel; and added, it is as true as the sun shines on that floor, and dim as my eyes are I see that . . .

Lillias Adie died in prison and was buried within the seamark at Torryburn.—WEBSTER, pp, 27-34.

[For the trials of other Torryburn witches—Elspeth Williamson, Jean Neilson, Agnes Currie, Mary Wilson and Helen Kay—see WEBSTER, p. 34; CHAMBERS (2) vol. iii. pp. 298-9.]

1704. *Pittenweem.*—Peter Morton, smith at Pittenweem, being desired by one Beattie Laing to do some work for her, which he refused, excusing himself in respect he had been pre-engaged to serve a ship with nails, within a certain time, so that till he had finished that work, he could not engage in any other; that notwithstanding, the said Beattie Laing declared herself dissatisfied and vowed revenge. The said Peter Morton, afterward being indisposed, coming by the door, saw a small vessel full of water, and a coal of fire slockened in the water; so perceiving an alteration in his health, and remembering Beattie Laing's threatenings, he presently suspects devilry in the matter, and quarrels the thing. Thereafter, finding his indispositions growing worse and worse, being tormented and pricked as if with bodkins and pins, he openly lays the blame upon witchcraft, and accuses Beattie Laing. He continued to be tormented, and she was by warrant apprehended, with others in Pittenweem. No natural reason could be given for his distemper, his face and neck being dreadfully distorted, his back prodigiously rising and falling, his belly swelling and falling on a sudden; his joints pliable, and instantly so stiff, as no human power could bow them. Beattie Laing and her hellish companions being in custody, were brought to the room where he was; and his face covered, he told his tormentors were in the room, naming them. And though formerly no confession had been made, Beattie Laing confessed her crime, and accused several others as accessory.—The said Beattie having confessed her compact with the devil, and using of spells; and particularly her slockening the coal in water; she named her associates in revenge against Peter Morton, viz. Janet Corset, Lillie Wallace, and Lawson, had framed a picture in wax, and every one of the forenamed persons having put their pin in the picture for torture. They could not tell what become of the image, but thought the devil had stolen it, whom they had seen in the prison.—Beattie Laing likewise said, that one Isobel Adams, a young lass, was also in compact with the devil. This woman was desired to fee with Beattie, which she refused: and Beattie let her see a man at the other end of the table, who appeared as a gentleman, and promised her all prosperity in the world: she promised her service to him; and he committed uncleanness with her, (which she said no other had done before) and he put his mark in her flesh, which was very painful. She was shortly after ordered to attend the company to go to one McGrigor's house to murder him. He awakening when they were there, and recommending himself to God, they were forced to withdraw. This Isobel Adams appeared ingenuous and very penitent in her confession; she said, he who forgave Manasseh's witchcrafts, might forgive hers also; and died very penitent, and to the satisfaction of many.

This Beattie Laing was suspected by her husband, long before she was laid in prison by warrant of the Magistrates. The occasion was this; she said, that she had packs of wool coming from Leith to her, which she was to sell at Auchtermuchty fair; and they being longsome in coming to the market, he said, "It would not be in time for the fair." She desired him to go to the market, for she was sure her merchant would not fail her. He went off long before her; and when he came to the town, he found her before him, and two packs of very good wool, which she instantly sold; and coming home with a black horse which she had with her, they drinking till it was late in the night ere they came home, the man said, "What shall I do with the horse?" She replied, "Cast the bridle on his neck, and you will be quit of him." And as her husband thought, the horse flew with a great noise away in the air.—They were, by a complaint to the Privy Council, prosecute by her Majesty's Advocate 1704, but all set at liberty save one, who died in prison, in Pittenweem. Beattie Laing died undesired, in her bed, in St Andrew's; all the rest died miserable and violent deaths.—SINGLAR, pp. 257-260.

For "Additional Particulars," "A Just Reproof," etc., see SINCLAR, pp. xlviii-xcl; COOK, pp, 49-149; CHAMBERS (2), pp. 299-302; and cf. *infra*, p. 355.

Brunt Laft. *St. Monans.*—In the upper regions of the Kirk, accessible by a stair in the steeple, there was a certain peculiar recess called the "Brunt Laft." Respecting the origin of this title there is only one opinion extant. . . . During the benighted ages of superstition and priestly domination [!], numerous were the helpless victims that perished in the flaming faggots under the conviction of witchcraft; and St. Monans being much infested with such notable beings, was not behind in the discharge of its duty. The Kirk Hill was the arena where such flagrant exhibitions formerly took place; the beadle being the principal executioner. After the faggots were exhausted, his special duty was to scatter the ashes towards the four winds of heaven, and to deposit the burnt fragments of the bones in the recess before mentioned in order to record the transaction. Hence it was denominated the "Brunt Laft."

This barbarous practice, however, may be said to have been totally annihilated by King James's ingenious method of proving witches, namely, when any one was accused of being uncanny, she was put in a balance against the family Bible, and her preponderance was the proof of her innocence; because the Bible, being the Word of God, was more than sufficient to outweigh all the works of the devil; and she was accordingly acquitted.—JACK, pp. 136-137.

FOOTNOTES:

[1] This is the earliest existing case in the Records of the High Court, of this nature; and it is almost the only instance of so mild a sentence having been pronounced. [The culprit was perhaps a Gypsy.]

[2] Care.

[3] Neckcloth, cravat.

[4] Moreover.

[5] Moist heat (?)

[6] Delivered.

[7] Afraid.

[8] Examine.

[9] *Poustie, polestas.*

[10] The brownies or fairies, and the Queen of Faery (*q.d.* elf-hame?).

[11] Grandfather's son, paternal uncle. He is called "hir cousing and moder-brotheris-sone" above.

[12] "Ane carling of the Quene of Phareis,
That ewill-win yeir to Elphyne careis,
Through all Braid-Albane scho hes bene,
On horsbak on Hallow-ewin;
And ay in seiking certayne nyghts,
As scho sayis, with sur sillie wychtis;
And names out nychtbouris sex or sewin,

That we belevit had bene in heawin.
Scho said scho saw thame weill aneugh,
And speciallie gude *Auld Balcleugh*
The *Secretare* and sundric vther;
Ane Williame Symsone hir mother brother,
Whom fra scho hes resavit a buike,
For ony herb scho lykis to luike:
It will instruct hir how to tak it;
In saws and sillubs* how to mak it;
With stones that mekill mair can doe,
In Leich-craft, whair scho layis them toe.
A thowsand maladies scho hes mendit,
Now being tane and apprehendit,
Scho being in the Bischopis cure,
And keipit in his Castell sure,
Without respect of Warldie glamer,
He past into the Witchis chalmer."
Legend of the Bischop of St. Androis, p. 321.
* Salves and potions.

[13] Cups or goblets.

[14] *Poustie, potestas,* viz. took the power of her left side from her.

[15] Discoloured and ill-looking.

[16] Worse.

[17] "In the hinder end of Harvest, on All-Hallowe'en,
    When our Good-neighbours does ride, if I read richt,
Some buckled on a bunewand and some on a bean,
    Ay trottand in troups from the twilight;
Some saidled a she-ape, all grathed into green,
    Some hobland on a hemp-stalk, hovand to the hight;
The King of Pharie and his Court, with the Elf Queen,

> With many elfish Incubus was ridand that night,
> There was an Elf on an ape, an wasel begat,
> Into a pot by Pomathorne;
> That brat chart in a busse was borne;
> They fand a monster on the morn,
> War faced nor a cat."
>
> *Flyling against Polwart*, Watson's Coll. Part iii, p. 12.

[18] Salves, ointments.

[19] Modern Scotch "fearsome," frightful.

[20] Terrified.

[21] Rated, scolded, threatened.

[22] Twenty weeks.

[23] Before the Court of Elfame.

[24] A tithe, or tenth part of them. This singular part of the prevailing superstition the Editor has seldom before met with. It suggests a strange idea of a kind of intermediate state of existence, maintained by the "guid nichtbouris," through the medium of evil spirits; and for this extraordinary privilege, they were annually *decimated*, or forced to pay tithe to "Sathanas," their lord paramount. The *wallydraigles* of this foul nest were no doubt pitched upon for payment of the annuity, and Maister Williame was jealous of the fate of his unfortunate relative, Alisoun. In the introduction to the *Tale of Young Tamlane*, Sir Walter Scott remarks, "This is the popular reason assigned for the desire of Fairies to abstract young children, as substitute for themselves in this dreadful tribute" (paying the teind to hell).

"Then I would never tire Janet,
  In Elfish land to dwell;
But aye at every seven years,
  They pay the teind to hell;
And I am sae fat and fair of flesh,
  I fear 'twill be mysel."

The Editor [*i.e.* Mr. Pitcairn] begs to refer the reader to the Essay "On the Fairies of Popular Superstition," in *The Border Minstrelsy*, edit. 1821, vol. ii. p. 109.

[25] Every.

[26] The celebrated Patrick Adamson, Archbishop of St. Andrews.

[27] Fever and ague.

[28] Palpitation at the heart?

[29] Weakness in the back and loins.

[30] Probably the flux.

[31] Salve.

[32] Ewe-milk.

[33] Perhaps the herb woodruff?

[34] Sodden.

[35] A pretty decent draught for an archbishop! . . . In that cutting satire, *The Legend of the Bishop of St. Andrews*, his trafficking with witches is thus recorded:

"Sic ane seiknes hes he tane,
That all men trowit he had bene gane
For leitchis mycht mak no remeid,
Thair was na bute to him bot deid.
He seing weill he wald nocht mend,
For Phetanissa hes he send.
With Sorcerie and Incantationes,
Raising the Devill with invocationes
With herbis, stanis, bukis and bellis,
Menis memberis and south-runing wellis;
Palme-croces and knottis of strease,
The paring of pricstis auld tees.
And *in principio* socht out fyne,
That vnder ane alter of stane had lyne
Sanct Jhones nutt and the four-levit claver,
With taill and mayn of a baxter aver
Had careit hame heather to the oyne,
Cuttit off in the cruik of the moone;
Halie water and the lamber beidis,
Hyntworthe and fourtie vther weidis;
Whairthrow the charming tuik sic force,
They laid it on his fat whyte horse.
As all men saw, he sone deceisit;
Thair Saga slew ane saikles beast.
This wald not serve; he sought ane vther,
Ane devill duelling in Anstruther
Exccading Circes in conceatis,
For changene of Wlisses mcatis," &c.
"Heiring how Witches wrang abust him,
The Kirkmen calld him and accused him,
And scharplie of theis pointis reproved him,
That he in Sorceric bcleavit him,
Whairthrow his saule mycht come to skaith,
The Witche and he confessing bayth,
Scho tuik some part of white wyne dreggis,

Wounded rayne and blak hen eggis,
And made him droggis that did him gude," &c.
DALYELL'S *Scottish Poems*, ii. 318.

[36] Parsley.

[37] Young onions.

[38] Comfrey.

[39] Wormwood.

[40] Elecampane.

[41] Probably cochlearie, the well-known and greatly prized scurvy-grass.

[42] In 1603, James Reid, who professed to be able to cure "all kynd of seiknes" was "wirrcit at ane staik," and burnt to ashes, on the Castle-hill of Edinburgh. He was convicted of meeting with the devil, "quhyles in the liknes of a man, quhyles in the liknes of a hors, . . . quhilk lykwayis lernit him to tak southe rynnand-watter to cuir the saidis diseissis." (Pitcairn, vol. ii. pp. 421-422.) Pitcairn remarks; "This superstition still obtains, in many remote places of Scotland, where the virtues of such water are firmly believed in.

[43] Vomit.

[44] Agnes Melvill . . . may be identified as the second witch said to have been consulted by Patrick Adamson, and described by Sempill as:

"Ane devill duelling in Anstruther,
Exceading Circes in conceatits,
For changene of Wlisses meatis:
Medusa's craftis scho culd declair
In making eddars of her hair:
Medea's practicques scho had plane,
That could mak auld men young agane."
   DALYELL'S *Scottish Poems of the Sixteenth Century*,
    p. 319; FLEMING, p. 800.

[45] Blood and corrupted or purulent matter.

[46] Death.

[47] Clergyman of the parish of Newburgh.

[48] Strange, unreal, unaccountable.

[49] Crosses and signs.

[50] Shirt.

[51] Mad.

[52] A hasp of yarn is equal to twelve "*cuts*" or six "*heer.*" Each "*cut*" goes six score times round the reel.

[53] Epilepsy, or the falling sickness. Perhaps it may refer to consumption, "*decay*" or "*decline.*"

[54] Out of a small box or chest.

[55] Wrapping, *rolling*.

[56] Kine, cattle.

[57] Athwart, across.

[58] Which they had not yielded for the space of a month.

[59] Kinsmen, relations.

[60] Water-fowl.

[61] Little "beasts," Scotticé, for some sort of small birds or fowls, such as snipes, etc.

[62] A hole to be made in the north wall of the house.

[63] A live fowl.

[64] Backwards, contrary to the course of the sun.

[65] Arm-pit.

[66] To lay the woman's song seems to have been an emphatical phrase, formerly used as denoting the change of mirth to sorrow, for the loss of a husband or a lover.—JAMIESON'S *Dic.*

[67] A drink taken with a friend when one is about to part with him; as expressive of one's wishing him a prosperous journey, —JAMIESON'S *Dic.*

[68] Grass-rent.

[69] Disbursed.

[70] Had a war of words.

[71] Dwindled; declined in health.

[72] The beginning of Autumn.

[73] Gradually approach.

[74] A small proprietor; see "Fife laird," p.281.

[75] Spell.

[76] Witches were said to have had the power of making the milk of their neighbour's cow flow into their own vessels, by drawing or *milking* (as it was termed) a tedder in Satan's name, and circulating it in a contrary direction to the sun.

[77] Martinmas.

[78] Probably this was the *lucken gowen* (*i.e.* the closed or locked gowen) or globe flower. . . . It used to be in great repute with the country people as a charm.

[79] Cap, head covering.

[80] An allusion evidently here to one of the means supposed to be employed by witches in carrying out their malevolent designs—by exposing a waxen image of their victim to a slow fire, and thus causing in him by their incantations a similar wasting and decay.

[81] Same as rantle-tree.

[82] Seven grains of wheat.

[83] Salve or ointment.

[84] Barley-seed.

[85] Also written *withershins* or *widdershins*, in a contrary direction to the sun.

[86] Brainpan, head.

[87] Howling.

[88] Road.

[89] Grief.

[90] Certain officials of the catchpole species, who, at that period, were annually appointed by the feuars, as conservators of the peace.

[91] This was a sort of wooden instrument somewhat in shape of a paddle, having the flat end stuck full of pins. This instrument was occasionally brought into collison with various parts of her body, in order to keep the witch moving, that sleep might be effectually prevented.

[92] Torch or match.

[93] Weaned.

[94] Presbytery.

[95] The desire to ascertain whether the accused has been guilty of renunciation of baptism, explains the persistence of the questioning as to the names by which the Devil was supposed to have called them, the presumption being that if they were habitually called by a name not given to them in Christian baptism, they could only have received that new name from Satan after renunciation of the baptism by the Church.—Dr. Joseph Anderson, *Pro. Soc. Ant. Scot.* vol. xxii. p. 244.

Printed in Great Britain
by Amazon

57620107R00040